W9-BJC-256

THIS LAND CALLED AMERICA: **IDAHO**

CREATIVE EDUCATION

Published by Creative Education

P.O. Box 227, Mankato, Minnesota 56002

Creative Education is an imprint of The Creative Company

www.thecreativecompany.us

Book and cover design by Blue Design (www.bluedes.com)

Art direction by Rita Marshall

Printed in the United States of America

Photographs by Alamy (Mike Read), Corbis (Bettmann, PIERRE PERRIN/CORBIS SYGMA, Joseph Sohm/Visions of America), Getty Images (Altrendo Nature, Gary Benson, Ira Block, Steve Bly, Paul Chesley, Alfred Eisenstaedt/Time & Life Pictures, David R. Frazier, Darrell Gulin, Eddie Hironaka, Hulton Archive, Dawn Kish, Joanna McCarthy, Neal Mishler, OLIVIER MORIN/AFP, MPI, A. Y. Owen//Time Life Pictures, Bill Schaefer, Anthony Stewart/National Geographic, Stock Montage, Stan Wayman//Time Life Pictures, Karl Weatherly, Randy Wells)

Library of Congress Cataloging-in-Publication Data

Peterson, Sheryl.

Idaho / by Sheryl Peterson.

p. cm. — (This land called America)

Includes bibliographical references and index.

ISBN 978-1-58341-637-2

1. Idaho—Juvenile literature. I. Title. II. Series.

F746.3.P48 2008

979.6—dc22          2007005685

First Edition

9 8 7 6 5 4 3 2 1

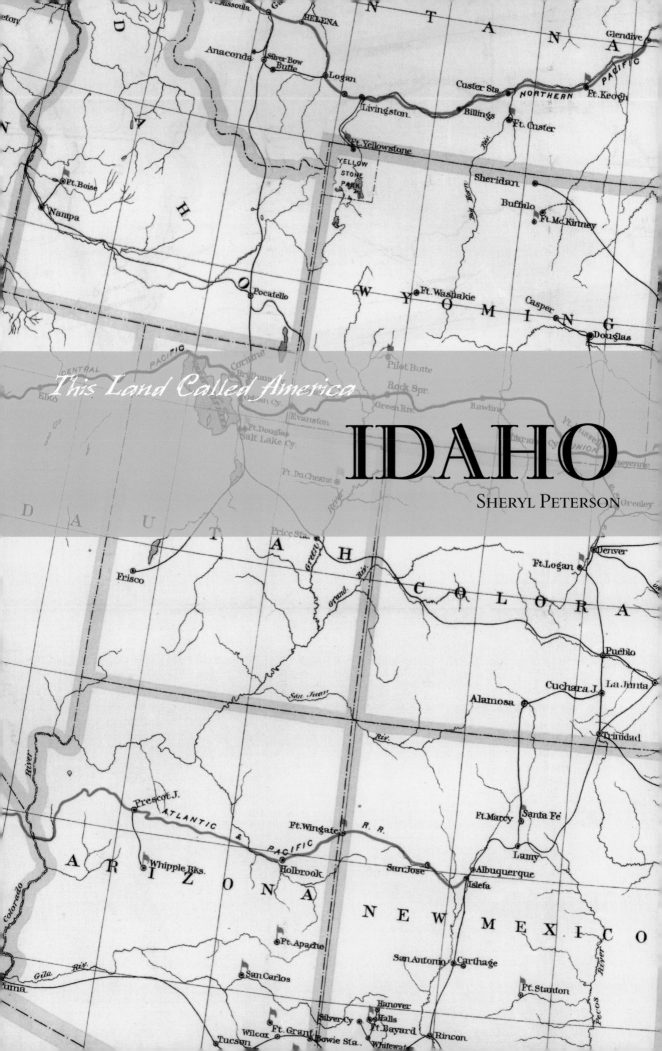

*This Land Called America*

# IDAHO

Sheryl Peterson

# Idaho

SHERYL PETERSON

WATER SPRAYS AND RUSHES PAST THE SIDES OF
THE RAFT. PEOPLE PULL HARD ON THEIR PADDLES.
THEY STEER AROUND JAGGED ROCKS. ONCE
THEY ARE PAST THE RAPIDS, THE RAFTERS FLOAT
SMOOTHLY AND ENJOY THE SCENERY. EVERY
SUMMER, PEOPLE TRAVEL TO IDAHO'S SNAKE AND
SALMON RIVERS. THEY NAVIGATE DOWN THE WILD
RIVERS, CRUISING BY HOT SPRINGS AND GRASSY
MEADOWS. SOMETIMES, PEOPLE SPY MOUNTAIN
GOATS, ELK, AND BLACK BEARS ON THE NEARBY
HILLSIDES. AFTER A THRILLING TRIP, THEY PULL
THEIR RAFTS UP ON SHORE. THE RIVER GUIDES
GRILL FRESH SALMON OVER THE CAMPFIRE, WHILE
THE VISITORS START PLANNING THEIR NEXT IDAHO
WHITE-WATER RAFTING ADVENTURE.

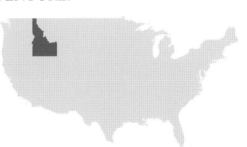

YEAR
1803 The U.S. purchases the Louisiana Territory, which includes Idaho.
EVENT

# Early Idaho

THE UNITED STATES WAS ESTABLISHED IN 1776. AT THAT TIME, IDAHO WAS STILL A WILD LAND WITH NO CABINS OR FARMS. IT WAS THE HOME OF MANY AMERICAN INDIANS, HOWEVER. THE SHOSHONI, BANNOCK, AND NEZ PERCE WERE THE MAIN TRIBES. THESE PEOPLE FISHED FOR SALMON IN THE RIVERS, HUNTED BUFFALO ON THE PLAINS, AND MADE CLOTHES AND MOCCASINS OUT OF ANIMAL SKINS.

*Before farmers could settle in Idaho (opposite), Sacagawea (left) led Lewis and Clark through the region to explore it thoroughly.*

*Sacagawea*

In 1803, President Thomas Jefferson sent men west to explore. Meriwether Lewis and William Clark traveled past the Mississippi River into Idaho. A brave Shoshoni woman named Sacagawea helped Lewis and Clark. She talked to her people, and the tribe members gave Lewis and Clark supplies and horses. Sacagawea showed Lewis and Clark the best places to cross the Rocky Mountains.

Lewis and Clark returned to the East Coast to report to President Jefferson. The explorers told of Idaho's tall mountains, swift rivers, and numerous animals. Soon, many trappers came to Idaho, and traders built trading posts.

YEAR
1805    Meriwether Lewis and William Clark enter Idaho at Lemhi Pass.
EVENT

- 7 -

# HO FOR THE YELLOW STONE

### AND ——— THE

# GOLD MINES
# OF IDAHO!

## A NEW AND VERY LIGHT DRAUGHT STEAMER WILL LEAVE

# SAINT LOUIS FOR BIGHORN CITY!

### THE JUNCTION OF BIGHORN AND YELLOW STONE RIVERS,

# SATURDAY, APRIL 2D, AT 12 O'CLOCK M.

Parties taking this route save 400 miles river transportation and over 100 miles land transportation. Bighorn City being by a good wagon road from Virginia City 200 and from Bannack City 205 miles.

## I WILL ALSO SEND TWO LIGHT DRAUGHT SIDE-WHEEL STEAMERS

# TO FORT BENTON

One leaving at the same time, and the second about fifteen days later. I am prepared to contract for Freight and Passage either to Bighorn City or Fort Benton.
refer to W. B. DANCE, JAS. STEWART and N. WALL, Virginia City, or to M. MANDEVILLE, Bannack City.

For Freight or Passage apply to **JOHN G. COPELIN,**

Care JOHN J. ROE & CO., St. Louis, Mo

Indians began trading furs for mirrors and necklaces. The Indians had never seen such things before. Sleek beaver furs were made into fancy hats and coats. People bought the fur clothing in city stores.

In 1836, missionaries Henry and Eliza Spalding came to Idaho with one of the first wagon trains to use the Oregon Trail. They built a mission near Lewiston and tried to turn the Nez Perce people into Christians. The Spaldings were the first white people to settle in Idaho. They showed the Indians how to dig ditches to irrigate, or water, their crops.

*The allure of the Homestead Act (below), coupled with the finding of gold (opposite), brought many people to Idaho in the 1860s.*

In the 1860s, settlers moved west. They came from the eastern states to Idaho. Other people traveled from England, Sweden, and Ireland. In 1862, President Abraham Lincoln passed the Homestead Act. The law stated that people could claim land in the West by building a home and living on the land for five years.

Pioneers rushed to Idaho to find farmland and claim the open spaces. The settlers worked hard. They cut down trees. They cleared the rough land and planted potatoes. Then they

YEAR
1810  Fort Henry, the first American trading post west of the Rocky Mountains, is built near St. Anthony.
EVENT

*After Idaho Indians such as the Nez Perce left their traditional lands, they were moved onto reservations.*

watered the dry land by digging ditches and laying pipes. When the settlers tried their luck at mining, they struck gold! Soon, thousands of eager miners flocked to the wild Idaho hills.

The city of Boise grew during the gold rush. The populations of Idaho City and Lewiston also doubled. But the big gold boom did not last long. Soon, the gold nuggets were all mined out, and people moved farther west in search of gold. Mining towns became "ghost towns." Stores and homes were left empty.

In the late 1860s, the U.S. government started telling the Idaho Indians to move to reservations. These were areas of land set aside for American Indians. The Indian tribes did not see why they should leave their homes, since they had helped to guide American settlers. The Indians fought against the U.S. Army, but they eventually lost and had to make the move.

Railroads were built across the Idaho wilderness. By 1890, more than 88,000 people lived in Idaho. On July 3, 1890, Idaho became the 43rd U.S. state. Colonel George L. Shoup served as the state's first governor before being elected to the U.S. Senate that same year.

*Silver City*

YEAR

1843    The first covered wagons to travel the Oregon Trail cross into Idaho.

EVENT

# Up High, Down Low

Northern Idaho is bordered by the province of British Columbia, Canada. The states of Washington and Oregon lie to the west. Parts of Nevada and Utah form the southern boundary. Wyoming and Montana touch Idaho's eastern side.

Parts of Idaho are still as rugged as they were in the days of Lewis and Clark. Some mountains are too steep to climb. Some lakes, located in inactive volcanoes, are too high up to reach.

Idaho has many different geographic features. The south is flat and dry. The west, east, and north have bare hills. Between the hills are areas of good farmland and many trees. The Rocky Mountains run through the middle of the state. The high, jagged peaks stretch from Idaho's northwestern panhandle to its southern border. The "panhandle" is the narrow part of the state that touches Canada.

Idaho has more than 200 tall mountain peaks. They rise 8,000 feet (2,438 m) or higher. Mount Borah, or Borah Peak, is the state's highest point at 12,662 feet (3,859 m). It was named after William E. Borah, Idaho's U.S. senator from 1907 to 1940. People hike to the top of Borah Peak, but they do not stay for long. There is no vegetation or water at that altitude.

*Although not a peak or part of Idaho's mountain chain, Balanced Rock is a unique formation.*

On other Idaho mountains, bears, goats, and bighorn sheep climb and feed. Herons, whistling swans, and eagles fly overhead. Mountain lakes and rivers are filled with salmon and rainbow trout.

YEAR

**1860**  Thirteen Mormon families found Franklin, the first permanent settlement in Idaho.

EVENT

Т he Snake River cuts through a gigantic gorge called Hells Canyon. It is the deepest canyon in North America— deeper even than Arizona's Grand Canyon. The narrow gorge runs for nearly 70 miles (113 km). People enjoy camping, hiking, and rafting in Hells Canyon. A dazzling waterfall called Shoshone Falls drops 212 feet (65 m) down into the Snake. The waterfall, located near the city of Twin Falls, is higher than New York's famous Niagara Falls.

The Salmon River has been called the "River of No Return." Powerful currents shuttle canoes downstream. But the currents are too strong for people to paddle back upstream. Instead, people have to ride in speedy jet boats to get back up the Salmon River.

*The sport of fly fishing is popular in Idaho (above), but even the adventurous would not want to fish in the powerful Snake River, which runs through Hells Canyon (opposite).*

1863    Idaho becomes a territory on March 4, with Lewiston as its capital.

*The soaring Teton Mountains of Wyoming can be seen from Idaho, as they are just across the border.*

*Teton Mountains*

Idaho has rich deposits of ores such as gold, silver, lead, and zinc. In the canyons and deserts, people sometimes find a star garnet, the state gem. Agates, rubies, and jade are found in the Idaho hills. Idaho has more than 72 other kinds of gemstones. Only the continent of Africa has more!

Forests cover about one-third of Idaho and produce much of America's lumber and paper products. The state tree, the western white pine, is made into high-grade lumber. People use white pine to make smaller products such as matches and toothpicks.

Potatoes grow on the Columbia Plateau in southern Idaho. Idaho potatoes are world-famous. The town of Blackfoot calls itself the "Potato Capital of the World." Idaho farmers also produce wheat and sugar beets. Ranchers herd cattle for beef and raise dairy cows for milk.

Idaho's climate varies. Mountain areas are cooler, while southern Idaho is warmer and drier than the rest of the state. Parts of Idaho receive as much as 200 inches (508 cm) of snow each year. In the south, though, the average yearly precipitation is only 13 inches (33 cm).

*Some of Idaho's plentiful forests are cleared in a checkerboard pattern to provide lumber.*

YEAR
1866    Silver City is the first Idaho town to receive telegraph service.
EVENT

# Potatoes and People

IDAHO HAS FEWER PEOPLE THAN MOST U.S. STATES.
MORE THAN HALF OF ALL IDAHOANS LIVE IN OR NEAR
BOISE OR OTHER CITIES. IN THE LATE 1800S, FAMILIES
CAME FROM ENGLAND, IRELAND, AND GERMANY. STILL
OTHERS TRAVELED FROM SWEDEN, DENMARK, AND
NORWAY. THEY FARMED THE LAND, WORKED IN THE
SILVER MINES, OR LOGGED IN THE FORESTS. TODAY,

about 91 percent of Idahoans have European backgrounds.

Around 1895, people moved to the U.S. from the mountains of northern Spain, a region called the Basque. They came to find gold in lofty mountains that reminded them of home. After that, they became sheep ranchers in southern Idaho. Some started new businesses in Boise. Boise now has more Basque people than any other city in America.

Settlers also came to Idaho from other parts of the U.S. They drove wagons from the East Coast and rode on horseback from nearby Utah and California. Franklin was Idaho's

*Many people from Spain's Basque region became sheepherders (above) or settled into the business life of the capital city of Boise (opposite).*

*Downhill skier Picabo Street competed in the 2002 Winter Olympics, held in Salt Lake City, Utah.*

first real town. It was started by Mormons in 1860. Mormons are a Christian people who strictly follow the teachings of their group's founder, Joseph Smith.

Mexicans moved into Idaho, too. Today, Mexican Americans and other Hispanics make up about nine percent of Idaho's population. At one time, many American Indians lived in Idaho. Now, only one percent of Idaho's population is Indian. Many still live on the Nez Perce Reservation in northwestern Idaho.

No matter their background, most people in Idaho are active. Picabo Street is a world-famous Idaho skier. She was born in the small town of Triumph and was named Picabo after a nearby town. Street grew up without a TV and played outside with her seven brothers, learning to downhill ski very fast. Street won a silver medal at the 1994 Winter Olympics in Norway. Four years later, she won a gold medal in Tokyo, Japan.

YEAR
1874    On May 2, the first train from the East arrives in Franklin, Idaho.
EVENT

*The Clearwater River runs through the Nez Perce Reservation, which is also a national historical park.*

YEAR

**1890** Idaho becomes the 43rd state in the union on July 3.

EVENT

Harmon Killebrew was a well-known baseball player from
Idaho. He was born in Payette and played for the Minnesota
Twins from 1961 to 1974. Killebrew hit 573 career home runs
and was elected to the Baseball Hall of Fame in 1984.

Ketchum, Idaho, was the final home of famed writer Ernest
Hemingway. Hemingway loved to hunt pheasants and ducks in
the valleys and woods close to his home. He wrote novels such
as *For Whom the Bell Tolls* and *The Old Man and the Sea*.

Carol Ryrie Brink was another Idaho author. She was born
in Moscow, Idaho. Brink wrote *Caddie Woodlawn*, which tells
the story of Brink's grandmother's life as a pioneer. In 1936, the
book won the Newbery Medal, the highest honor a children's
book can receive.

*Harmon Killebrew
started playing for the
Washington Senators,
the team that became
the Minnesota Twins.*

YEAR

1906    The largest sawmill in the U.S. opens at Potlatch, Idaho.

EVENT

**A**bout half of the people in Idaho depend on farming to make a living. Some live on the farms and raise wheat and hay. Others process the crops or sell things that farmers need. Idaho is most famous, however, for one special potato called the Russet Burbank. Luther Burbank first grew the potato in the 1870s.

Some Idahoans are sheep and cattle ranchers. Some work in factories that make flour. Others process sugar and animal feeds. Factory workers also make computer parts. And many people work to help tourists have fun in their state.

*When Luther Burbank (above) was 21, he began experimenting with food. The Russet Burbank potato, now harvested from Idaho fields (opposite), was one of his earliest successes.*

YEAR

1934    Idaho becomes the nation's leading silver producer.

EVENT

# In Idaho Alone

IDAHO IS A PLACE WHERE MANY PEOPLE GO FOR EXCITING OUTDOOR ADVENTURES. PEOPLE CAN FLOAT ON A RAFT DOWN A RIVER. THEY CAN ZIP DOWN A SNOWY MOUNTAIN SKI SLOPE. OR THEY CAN HIKE, BIKE, AND CAMP IN IDAHO'S HILLS.

**LIFE**

SKI LIFT AT SUN VALLEY

MARCH 8, 1937 **10** CENTS

The first ski resort in the U.S. was built near Ketchum, Idaho. Union Pacific railroad man and skier Averell Harriman opened Sun Valley in 1936. He wanted to create a place in America that would rival the ski resorts in Europe. Harriman modeled his upscale resort after an Austrian village.

Sun Valley famously featured the world's first mountain chairlift. Each winter, hundreds of skiers continue to ride the chairlifts up Mount Baldy. During the summer, famous figure skaters such as Scott Hamilton and Michele Kwan spin and jump for the crowds at the Sun Valley outdoor ice rink.

*Some areas of Idaho are better suited to building ski resorts such as Ketchum's Sun Valley (represented above) than for farming (opposite).*

Since Idaho has no professional sports teams, fans support their college teams. Boise State University's football team, the Broncos, was the 2007 Tostitos Fiesta Bowl champion. The University of Idaho Vandals and the Idaho State Bengals also thrill spectators in sports such as basketball and swimming.

About 50 miles (81 km) southeast of Ketchum is the Cra-

Craters of the Moon National Monument affords a rare chance for people to walk on volcanic craters.

ters of the Moon National Monument. Lava, the hot melted rock from a volcano, once flowed there. Over time, the lava hardened into huge holes called craters. The area looks a lot like the surface of the moon—dry and rocky, with no plant life. Astronauts planning to go to the moon have trained at the park to get used to the stark environment.

Not far from Ketchum, it is possible to walk on top of two rivers. The waters of the Big River and Little Lost River flow into the lava fields and disappear. From there, the water travels hundreds of miles under the ground. Finally, at Thousand Springs, the water pours out through holes in the walls of the Snake River Canyon.

Lava also created the Shoshone Indian Ice Caves. The cave floors are coated with layers of thick ice. This ice is present even on warm summer days. Another chilly place is the Crystal Ice Cave near Pocatello. Inside the cave, visitors can see a giant, frozen waterfall.

Fly fishermen know that Idaho's Silver Creek has some of the best trout fishing in the country.

YEAR

1942  Japanese Americans are placed in a camp near Eden, Idaho, during World War II.

EVENT

YEAR
1992     Linda Copple Trout becomes the first woman appointed to the Idaho Supreme Court.
EVENT